Not Done Yet…
Memories & Other
Thoughts

Noreen Gelling

Not Done Yet…Memories & Other Thoughts
Noreen Gelling
Copyright © 2011 Noreen Gelling
Published by Jukiro Creative

The names in this book are fictional, the feelings and memories real.

ISBN 978-0615592084

Dedication

This book is dedicated to the parents I miss, the brothers & sisters I love, the children in my life I adore, the friends I need; and my life partner and soul mate who has been the touchstone in my life for nearly three decades.

Table of Contents

Preface

I have always written. From as far back in my life as I can remember I wrote poems, stories, random sentences that never went anywhere. This is the start of actually putting my writing together and sending it out to the world. I don't know where it will land. I am hoping it strikes somewhere around your heart and helps you awaken something in yourself that calls you to a better place, forgotten memory or inspiration for tomorrow.

Some pieces contained herein are longer, but not necessarily more important. They just needed more words. May they fall gently.

Chapter One

Motherhood

There is no way of knowing really, where life will lead. You make your best choices each day and then move on from there. Some days are more successful than others, I guess. Sometimes I think about the varied paths I have walked, and I do an inward shudder at the thought of the place I am in today. Not because it is a "bad" place, but because I simply cannot imagine my life any other way than it is. Maybe not so much than it is, than who is in it. I listen to the boys running around the driveway, laughing yelling wildly swinging a golf club at a soccer ball back and forth back and forth. It is one of their created combo games, soco-golf. They swing; Michael rides his just too small trike around in the madness. I am anticipating that someone will come in the back door crying after having been clocked with a club. I will need to explain well that's what happens when you play like boys, you win some, you lose some, and some get rained out in a river of tears.

What brought me here? I never thought it would be this way. How can life be so full of life itself, when you least expect it? How does someone such as me deserve the someone's they are and are constantly becoming. I don't know. I sometimes feel as though I am just an honored guest of their journey. That I somehow slipped, or took a wrong turn and landed on their path. Surely their souls sought me out, or drew me in to the journey, for in and of myself, I could not have earned it. Could I have?

Motherhood. Not just garden variety motherhood, adoptive motherhood. It is all the same and it is so much different. When a child is created and carried in the womb, the missing, different ingredient is randomness. I so often wonder about the randomness of us as a family. I look at them, each of them, and I understand the gift of spirit called wonder and awe. They take my breath away. Sometimes I watch them when they sleep, so peaceful, so beautiful. I wonder, and I am in awe of the twists of fate, or the plan from forever that brought us together.

I remember so well the first time I saw each of their faces. Just one of a dozen faces on the computer screen. It was such an odd thing, looking at all the faces of all the children. The instant you see yours, you know them. I tell people that my heart literally skipped a beat in knowing when I saw them. They look at me as if I am strange. I imagine they think I am making it up, or romanticizing an otherwise uneventful moment. Yet it is true. There is no doubt, no shred of hesitation in my mind, heart or soul that they were born for me. Randomly?

It was just seven months after my father died; just 18 months after we buried my mother. Life seemed to just be getting back to normal, well, as normal as life can be after your world crumbles from beneath your feet. Losing them, walking them both to the gates of heaven, was both the greatest honor, and greatest heartbreak of my life, twice over in eighteen short months. It shifted my world off its otherwise steady rotation. I was just getting back to steady, back to work, back to routine. I tried every day to remember not to reach for the phone to call them. I was working hard to push my way through things that used to seem so important but in the shadow of the pain seemed so meaningless. Forever my life was marked as before and after.

It was January; we had come through Thanksgiving and Christmas without them. We were still breathing. It was a normal gray day and as I pulled into the driveway Kate said I think we could raise a kid, T chimed in from the backseat, "hell yeah." Really? A kid, now? Adopt now? Really? The thought spun around my head for a bit, and someplace it found a root in my soul.

We had talked about adoption before, looked into the requirements and commitments. It was too much. Too much for us to take on, kids with disabilities and histories. We feared we would not be able to give them what they needed; afraid they would take what we didn't even know we had to give. We were resigned to the joys of the nieces and nephews, of which there were plenty. But this time, this simple conversation, took root. I remember how the conversation started in the car that day. A little girl joined the school I was principal of at the time. She was one of the last children allowed out before the United States closed adoptions from Cambodia. She was beautiful, she was sweet, and she was seven. In her we saw the possible, and in us we felt the pull. We talked and talked and talked for weeks it seemed. We scoured the internet for information. Compared programs, China? No. We had decided boy. Russia? No. The time requirement was too long in country. Guatemala? YES! Really? Guatemala? Yes. The children were in private foster care, the time required in country was manageable, the people were warm, and the flight was short. We started combing the agency lists.

We filed with the government for permissions and visas. We found a home study social worker. We had begun a journey that I could not have imagined.

We did everything the "wrong "way. We fell in love with a picture of two brothers, and that agency became our agency. We sent thousands of dollars before we had checked out a single reference. It did not matter; we had pictures of two little boys, ages 3 and 5 who were going to be our sons. The process dragged on for months, we were fingerprinted, we filed more papers, and we sent more money. We waited, and waited and waited. In early August the agency gave us the bad news; the birthmother had decided to take them back. It happens she said, but not to worry we could pick two more children from the website. Pick? Are you kidding me? This was not about "picking" this was about love and hopes and dreams. We were devastated. After a week or so of tears and broken spirits, we got an e-mail from the agency, please look at the photo of the boy Carlos, he is perfect for you. We looked. He was cute, it was not him. We scrolled down the page, there, there they were, one photo above the other. Juan with the sweetest smile in the world was five, and he was ours. Xavier with the glint in his eye was three, and he was ours. We just knew.

I called the agency, yes they were both available, and yes we could adopt them. Are we sure we did not want Carlos? Yes, we have our sons. Faxes and e-mails flew, the process had begun again. It was November, the process was slow and the lies from the agencies kept coming. The papers were stolen, the car was broken into, and the attorney was on vacation. Time dragged and dragged, our hopes for Christmas were fading fast. We set our sights on Easter boys. I went to the website to get the address one more time to mail some copy of something else that seemed lost or misplaced. As I opened the site, I saw his face, his smile, and my heart literally jumped for the third time. He was mine. I told Kate we had another son waiting for us, he was seven months old. No. Three is too many, she was too old for an infant, the cost was too high, and three boys was a crazy idea. Just look at his picture, no. Please? No. We can do this Kate, really we can, just look at his picture. She looked. Her heart jumped too. Diego was ours. More paper work, more faxes, more money, more e-mails. Christmas came and went. Valentine's Day came and went, more pictures arrived, and more lies were told. I could not stand it anymore. I told the agency we were going to Guatemala over Easter, we wanted the DNA testing done, and things moving. When I told her we were going, amazingly things start moving. We booked our flights. I could not believe we were actually going to Guatemala. It was a place I had never given thought too, let alone visit, nor be forever linked to via my sons. We shopped and shopped and shopped. We packed suitcases that were way too heavy, and had hearts that were way too full. We were full, too full; of hope, of promise, of joys, of our boys. They all had birthdays; they were now six, four and one. With determination of spirit, and tickets in hand, a strange feeling crept into the process. What if? What if they did not like me? What if I had been wrong in reading my own soul about this decision, what if I couldn't? What did I know about being a mother? What if I had not learned enough from my own? How did she do it? How did she learn to love and give and embrace five of us? How did she manage? What if this was all a big fantasy that had spun out of control? My fears were so deep, and anxiety growing so high, I sometimes caught myself holding my breath. What if?

We landed in Guatemala City at 6:20 pm local time on Good Friday, 2003. It was such a strange and delightful feeling to be in a foreign land on such a pursuit. Everything was so different, the sounds of the traffic and people, the lights on the streets, it was all so different and being there so surreal. I felt as though I were watching myself in a dream. Neither of us spoke enough Spanish to hold a two minute conversation, but here we were in the back seat of a car speeding through Guatemala City with two strangers the agency sent to be our guides. Off we rode into a place our hearts would never come back from.

They told us the foster mothers would bring the boys to the hotel lobby Saturday morning at 10:00 AM. We checked in, we unpacked; we managed to order food at the restaurant. The minutes ticked, the anxiety and excitement grew.

I fell asleep studying the word and phrase list I had created. Everything I could think of that we might need to communicate to a six and four year old over five days. Do you need a bathroom? Are you hungry? Do you want to play? It is time for sleep. Hold my hand. I love you: Te amo. We did not know what to expect; but we were here.

After our travels, we should have slept till noon, or at least not be awake hours before the wakeup call we had scheduled for 8 a.m. We gulped coffee, we ate breakfast, we paced, we went for a walk, we paced. We walked into the lobby at around 9:45. I saw him across the lobby, I thought I would melt. I think I floated across the lobby to him.

The foster mother smiled as she handed him to Kate, we spoke a few words thanking God for her limited English. Kate handed him to me, I held my baby for the first time. He put his hand on my cheek and smiled. I felt the full force of an indescribable love. I had a new before and after moment in my life.

Shortly after ten a tall austere woman arrived with a shy little boy in a red shirt following behind her. He looked so small and afraid. He carried a sip cup, and kept his head down. He did not smile, he did not talk, and he stood perfectly still. He looked at us through his huge black brown eyes. I wonder what he was looking for. In retrospect I imagine he was trying to make sense of where he was, of who we were, of what was happening. When it was time for the foster mother to leave, he did not seem to care that she left. He took my offered hand and held it tighter than I anticipated. We walked to the elevator and into a life he could not have imagined, from a life he would not have survived.

As we talked through one foster mother to the other, a group arrived with our third son; he was carrying roses clearly clipped from a wild garden. He reached out to us and smiled a very nervous smile. Someone had told him this was happening but not why. He allowed us to take pictures of him, he kept smiling. He was not happy to see the foster family leave. He did not cry, but he looked as though he might. Kate held his hand and gave him an extra hug. He needed reassurance. A hug was all it took before the smile returned and his heart clicked back to its seemingly permanent state of happy enough.

That night as they slept I watched them, watched them until every "what if" dissipated from my heart, soul and mind forever. I had doubts about many things, but never again did I doubt whether or not I could love them enough. We spent six days together swimming, eating, laughing, playing, trying to communicate, and hugging. Doing all the things we needed to do to nurture the thread of love that would and does continually knit us together as a family.

Leaving them was heart wrenching. Our only solace was that we would be back to bring them home forever in a few short months, so we thought.

We thought we would be spending bright summer days together exploring their new world. We went back to Guatemala in June, but it was not a pick up trip. By June the controversy over the Hague Treaty was in full swing. Powers wanted to stop all cases in progress, and have them all become "Hague Compliant." Other groups, attorneys, agencies, were fighting to process adoptions started.

Misinformation and confusion was exported each day via the internet and newspapers. We, along with hundreds of others waiting for their children were in a constant state of high alert panic. No one knew for sure whether or not they would ever hold their children again. We hung on; I could not allow myself to believe we had come so far, to have to walk away. The agency advised us not to visit again, to wait. We ignored her. It had been ten weeks since we left Guatemala; we had to see them again. I had to feel my son wrap his hands around my shoulders and gently fall asleep. I had to see the smile close up, and look into their eyes. We left the day after school closed for the summer, with suitcases full of clothes, toys, shoes and hope. I remember wondering out loud if they would remember us, or if we would have to become re-acquainted all over again. That question was quickly answered. We were pacing around the hotel lobby waiting for the foster mothers, each 3-5 seconds I looked down the wide passage to the front doors. Finally, I saw Xavier coming through the huge glass doors. I started for them, he saw me and broke from the clutch of the foster mother, running the thirty feet or so to me. He leapt into my arms with such joyful force he nearly knocked me over. He hugged my neck, he smiled, he remembered. The five of us spent ten wonderful days together. They went back to their temporary homes. We left Guatemala more in love, more determined, and more convinced of the forever bonds started in a still photograph almost a year previous.

The weeks home dragged, the information around the Hague continued to spin us in a constant state of confusion. No adoptions were being processed. Cases were at a standstill and no one knew if or when the processes would start again, and if they did, when or for whom. Some rumor mongers said all adoptions started before a certain date would definitely "get out." Others said all cases would be reviewed and many would be rejected. Still others claimed it would all work out fine, this was just a temporary glitch the government needed to work out. I went with this group.

I had to stand with the believers, it was too hard to even let myself imagine they were not ours, would never be home. I held on to the belief that the challenge would work, the courts would rule in favor of allowing the started adoptions to continue, and quickly. It was not quickly. By the third week in August, we still did not know, but we had to see you again. We had two weeks before school started for us again, we found a flight, shopped, and left.

We had another great re-union in that hotel lobby. Diego was 17 months old now, much to the dismay of the foster mother, we taught him to walk during the week. It was such a joy to be there as he took his first steps, and smiled so proudly at himself doing so. The week was full of warm laughter and tight hugs, and it was coming to an end.

On day six we waited in the lobby for the foster mothers to pick you up. Watching each of them leave with Diego and Juan was heart breaking. We worked hard not to let you see us cry as we hugged and said goodbye. We sat with Timothy waiting. The minutes ticked, he sat on my lap and fell asleep. I stared down at that face wondering how long. How long before I never had to say goodbye again. He remained sleeping as the foster mother arrived, he did not wake when I carried him through the lobby and out the doors to the waiting taxi. Just as well I thought. He won't see me cry. As I handed him to the foster mother he woke up startled. He screamed, was crying, and reaching for me as she bent into the cab clutching him. As the taxi pulled away I could hear him crying through the open windows, and he would never know how each of those tears cut into my soul.

I was breathless with the pain. The memory of him reaching and crying for me, "No, mama, no" haunts me still. We left Guatemala balancing the delectation of the memories and the anguish of not knowing when or how this journey would end.

School began, time dragged, agency lies continued, rumors of Hague "news" continued. Finally, the official word came. The courts in Guatemala decided adoption as it was would continue; the cases in process would be finalized. Our jubilance overflowed, you were at long last, coming home.Unfortunately, the court decision and the predictions for all children to be home by Halloween had not taken into account the actual mess lying on the floor of the government office in the form of case files. It had not taken into account the passive anger of the processors who were ordered to work, but not held to a timeline. The cases began moving, at a torturous crawling pace. October churned on, still stinging from the memory of Xavier crying as the taxi pulled away, I needed to hear his voice. Needed to let him hear my voice, and hope that my poor Spanish was enough for him know I was still real. I dialed the number for the foster mother's house, after some difficult explaining, they put Xavier on the phone.

"Hola Xavier, es mami, Como estas?" All I heard was "Hola Mami, cuando eres que viene aqui?" When are you coming here? He did not know that in my heart, I had never left. I will be there soon my son, soon; but not soon enough.

By mid-November we were desperate for information, for help. We had pretty much given up on the agency ever giving us a straight answer. Somewhere along the line, I had obtained the phone number for the government office responsible for processing and ultimately approving adoptions. I had been calling weekly since August to a woman named Maria, who by mid November recognized my voice. I don't know what angel, or force of love from our mothers in heaven made this phone call, this week, different. Maybe it was the edge of desperation in my voice, maybe it was my consistent calls, but this time she asked me "Senora Noreen, do you trust your attorney?" A flat and quick "No" was my response.

I went on to tell her I had given up on the agency, I was on my own and determined. She gave me the name and phone number of a woman who might help me translate if I decided to come to Guatemala to speak with the officials myself. I thanked her. I hung up, we talked.

Go to the government and plead my case? What if it did not work? What if it backfired? What if, what if, what about….none of it mattered. We had to go to Guatemala, and did so determined to not leave without our sons. I called the number she gave me. An angel named Sophia assured me if I came to Guatemala she would make an appointment with the "officials."

I made an appointment to meet her in Guatemala City Monday morning.

It was Friday afternoon; I booked our flights with an open return date. I called my principal and explained I would not be in on Monday, or next week. I did not know when I would be back, but I had to go fight for my kids. She wished me Godspeed. I called the agency and told her we were headed back to Guatemala, I wanted my sons at the hotel Monday afternoon. She tried to convince me against this trip. Be patient she said. It had been twenty one months since we started the adoption process. Patience was no longer an option. Being away from our sons was no longer bearable. We left on Sunday, to begin what would become a five week odyssey of the heart.

Sophia arrived right on time Monday. We told her our long tired story and showed her pictures of our sons. She listened patiently, and asked us to trust her. She left with an envelope full of her fee, and all our hopes and dreams. The boys arrived later that day; it felt so good to hold them, to look into their smiling eyes. It had been almost three months since we had seen each other. Somewhere in the midst of the re-union I realized how happy they were to see each other again, they had begun the process of becoming "real" brothers.   With their hugs for each other, my spirit was rejuvenating, and my deepest dream was that this time would be the last time for a re-union. Our room phone rang Tuesday afternoon. Sophia had been to PGN, Diego and Xavier's case files were there. She had located the examiners, and the director of the agency would see me on Friday morning. I had just about 72 hours to prepare myself to plead for my sons. Most of that preparation took the form of a constant stream of prayer, as we walked, swam, ate, played, and kissed them goodnight, we prayed. I needed the words, needed the strength, and needed the miracle.

It was Thanksgiving Day in the USA, and we as we ate a full turkey dinner in the hotel restaurant, it was both thanks-giving, and miracle asking day.

On Friday morning I left Kate and the boys to breakfast and Teletubbies broadcasting in Spanish. I had donned my best catholic school girl looking outfit, and headed out the door with my heart pounding and spirit strong. This was going to work; this had to work. I walked with Sophia into the director's office with the full force of our family, our online adoption group, and Saint Michael behind, within and around me. At the desk sat a stern looking woman; not the director, the director's wife. She smiled, invited us to sit, and listened patiently as Sophia pleaded my case and showed her photos of the home and family waiting for them. She looked from the pictures to me, to Sophia. Finally, she sat back, took a breath, and rattled of a series of sentences to Sophia. She stood, Sophia stood, I stood. Sophia was smiling as she said gracias, she extended her hand to me, I shook her hand, I smiled, and we walked out of the office. Sophia explained as soon as we were out of earshot that we would be going to the case workers desks. Once there she would deliver the message from the director to sign off their cases and bring them to her that afternoon.

I would never have to say goodbye to Xavier and Diego again. The rest of the time at the offices was a blur of listening to Sophia deliver instructions and trying to digest the reality of what just happened. When I returned to the hotel, I went straight out to the pool where Kate and the boys were waiting. Juan and Xavier were playing in the water, Diego slept in his stroller. When Kate saw me approach she walked toward me, and she must have read my face. She fell into my arms crying when I told her two were coming with us. "What about Juan?" she cried "What about Juan?"

His case was not approved; it could not be as it was not yet in their offices. We made desperate calls from Guatemala to the agency, Sophia spoke to the attorney, there simply was no way his file was to be completed in the week we thought we had until we went home. We could not bear to tell his gentle heart that his brothers were going home, but he was not. The foster mother was planning on picking him up on Sunday anyway, so we let her. We packed up all their things as we had done thrice before, and went to the lobby to wait. Saying goodbye to him this time was easier, this time we had hope. We knew we would be back, maybe six weeks at most the attorney promised.

Monday morning started a twenty day odyssey of another series of highs and lows. The director signed their paperwork. Signed, sealed and almost delivered, they were legally mine. We just needed the final signature of Xavier's birthmother. She was unavailable. Over the weekend she had been arrested and moved to what they were calling a "safe house" as she had evidently been witness to a murder.

Diego's papers were done; he was ready to be processed at the American embassy just as soon as we obtained his Guatemalan passport. The attorney told me to meet him at the passport office; he would attach the needed seal, and sign the final papers. I packed a makeshift diaper bag and climbed into a cab with my baby and took off for some unknown part of the city.

Arriving at the passport office was a bold reminder to me that I was not in New Jersey anymore. Armed guards patrolled this section of the city. The office was a locked storefront with more guards and semi-automatic rifles inside.

I knocked, they let me in, and I waited. The attorney was late, when he did arrive, he had me sign some papers, he signed the papers, an official stamped them and sent us upstairs. At this point the attorney told me to wait upstairs they will call my name. I started up; when I reached the top I was shown into a room where they took Diego's photo. They pointed my way out to a large waiting room. I looked around for the attorney. He was gone. Nice guy.

I went to the far end front of the room and sat. In what seemed like a very short time, they called my name. I went to the window and was presented with a passport. It was time to head back to the hotel. I had not really thought about that detail. On the go trip I simply stepped outside the hotel and a cab arrived via the doorman whistle. I guess somewhere I had assumed the attorney would at least stick around long enough to help me find a cab.

As the armed guard let me out of the office, I put on my best Brooklyn face, and hit the street. I must have been quite a sight carrying Diego down the block; with a big bag slung over my shoulder and a look of determination on my face. There had to be a cab somewhere. I walked a little bit, and saw a taxi stand one block further, I got there only to discover three cabs. No drivers. A woman selling fruit took pity on me, and asked "taxi?" "Si" said I and she disappeared around the corner. Just as I was deciding what direction to walk in, she reappeared with a sleepy looking older man who opened the back door to the cab and motioned me in.

I thanked the fruit woman by offering her some quetzals, she refused, I insisted. She smiled, we drove away. With the passport done, Diego was now, according to the Guatemalan government, legally and finally mine; on to the American Embassy tomorrow.

Much as I was not prepared for the crowds and guards around the passport office; I was also not prepared for the fortress and lines at the American Embassy. Stretched for blocks and blocks was a line of people, I would later find out waiting to get into the embassy in the hope for a visa to America. It was nine o'clock in the morning. How long had they been standing there I wondered.

Diego and I entered the embassy through the citizen gate, the metal detectors, and the guards. Finally to the waiting room, with fifty other hope filled families, we waited. We were interviewed, I was given a packet, told not to open it, it was to be handed in to immigration when we arrived in the US. When we arrived in the US. When.

After a short interview and fee payment Diego was ours. Ours according the Guatemalan government, ours now according to the US government. His name was now Michael, he was ours. It was a funny feeling to have two governments acknowledge in two days what I had known since I laid eyes on him fourteen months prior.

We had to continue the fight for Xavier. We were on the phone several times a day with the agency, with the facilitator, with the attorneys, with anyone who would listen to our pleas. We needed the birthmother's signature; they were trying to get it, maybe manana. Which we came to understand did not mean tomorrow, it just meant not today. There were many "not todays" as the days drifted toward Christmas. We watched and greeted families as they came and went with their children. We waited. We waited until December 15th. The papers were signed December 15th. With luck, on a wing and a prayer we would be home for Christmas.

Again I went to the passport office. This time I knew what to expect right down to the disappearing attorney, and fruit seller taxi lady. Xavier and I were at the American embassy early on the morning of December 19th. It was Friday; the embassy was closing at one pm for the holidays. I remember feeling the anxiety in the room rise as the government issued clock on the wall ticked. If our paperwork was not processed today, we would be in Guatemala until January third. There were forty four families at the embassy that morning; all of them with their children and their dreams. We waited and waited, we were interviewed, and we waited. At noon, an announcement was made, the embassy staff had agreed to stay until all the families were processed. We and our children would all be home for Christmas. A round of applause and a group sigh went up from the crowd now crying tears of relief and joy. Strangers cried and hugged each other, we were going home.

I plopped Xavier right up on the counter when they called our name; through the window I was handed the packet with his picture stapled to the outside, 'Es mio!" he exclaimed. "Si" I said through my tears. "Manana, the avion" Tomorrow we go home my Timothy.

That afternoon we went to the airline office booked our return and purchased two child seats. We would be leaving Guatemala on the seven AM flight. We would land in Houston at eleven, leave Houston at two, and land in New Jersey at six. We spent hours packing all we had brought, and bought. We had quite a cartful as we left the hotel that had become home at four AM. The sun was still rising over the volcano when we lifted off to forever.

Houston was easy except for the overfull cart of luggage being maneuvered by one while the other held on to Timothy and pushed Michael in the stroller. Timothy talked non-stop, rambling in Spanish all the way from Houston to Newark. I had no idea what he was saying, or feeling, I only knew that every once in a while he took my hand, and rested against me. I silently wondered if he understood, he would never have to ask again, "when are you coming here?" "Here" was to be wherever we were together.

I will never forget the moment we saw the entire family through the glass partitions at the airport. Those final 100 feet of our journey, are forever etched in my heart. Timothy landed in Joanne's arms and clung. He must have known intuitively he was safe from the crowd there. I fell into Chris' arms after saying to him, "this is my baby." We were home, after five weeks of days, and thousands of miles of emotion, we were home.

Six years later you come bounding down the stairs wearing camouflage shorts, horizontal striped shirt and that smile. "Happy Special Day, honey! I am glad to see you smiling, and I know it's your special day, but you cannot wear that outfit to school, those patterns do not match." "Aww I thought they did" you reply, and quickly turn to head up the stairs again. I watch you bounce down the hall and I have to smile.

Six years ago today you and I were on a plane headed from Guatemala City to Miami, to Newark, to forever. At long last one journey was over and another was just beginning. I flew to Guatemala alone to pick you up. Your brothers had been home for five months already. Each of the days between December twentieth and May first was a bittersweet torture for us. We were here, you were there and we had many moments of fearing we would never see you again. Yet, here you were bounding about the house in mismatched patterns.

I arrived in Guatemala on Sunday; they were supposed to bring you to me on Monday. We had employed the help of Sophia again, and through some miracle she had seen to it that your paperwork was ready. I expected it would be a quick trip, passport Tuesday, embassy Wednesday, home Thursday. I was almost right.

Monday I wandered around until noon waiting for you. When you had not arrived by one, I called the facilitator. Four o'clock he told me, I went to the mall. I came back, I paced, four o'clock came and went. At five I finally got in touch with the facilitator, they would be there in an hour. At some point in that hour Sophia and her husband arrived, we waited. Finally, the foster mother, the facilitator, and some unknown man arrived. Where were you? "Not coming" they said. They were not bringing you to me until they were paid the balance the agency in the US owed them. Back and forth, up and down, around and around the rapid conversation went in Spanish between them and Sophia. I could not even catch a word here and there, my spirit had gone somewhere else.

I paced around the lounge area we were in, leaving it to Sophia. Finally, the facilitator was on the phone, he handed the phone to the unknown man. More words I did not understand fell to the floor. He handed the phone to Sophia, then she to the foster mother and back to the facilitator again. Sophia came to tell me the agency was "willing" to send the money via the wires, it should be there in an hour, and then they would go get him. Just then, over Sophia's shoulders, through the glass doors of the grand hotel entrance I caught a glimpse of him. He was on the curb, standing with his back to me near some man who was clearly keeping an eye on him.

Something in me snapped. In a flash and a blur I was past Sophia and out the door, I did not realize her husband was on my heels. As I got to the other side of the doors he saw me 20 feet off and came running. I scooped him into my arms and turned back for the hotel as Carlos, caught the arm of the man following after me yelling in Spanish and spoke to him.

The armed guards posted around the hotel were interested in the scene; I suppose I could have been stopped by them too. I did not think about danger, police or consequences. I was running on instinct, I wanted my son. I kept a tight hold and went pushing through the doors. Inside he clung to me and cried, through his tears I could hear "No, mama, dinero, dinero." Sophia was with me as we sat, I brushed your tears and she translated and explained. It was ok, you could stay with me. We were alright. The money came; the foster mother, the facilitator, and their troop left without you. It had been a three hour ordeal. When we finally got to the room, you took a bath, and I had to throw the clothes they brought you in right into the hotel garbage. Why had they let you live in such a state of filth? Where was the suitcase of clothes I left you with five months ago?

The answer was simple enough; they never expected to leave you there with me. They thought the fight would be longer and harder with the agency. The angels had other plans.

The next four days each brought their own wrinkles: wrong date on your birth certificate, problem with my name affidavit at the passport office, a cranky interviewer at the embassy reporting they never had your paperwork from the US side. At each obstacle, I held you a little closer. You were so confused, but so happy. When we were not running from one agency to the next we played at the pool, walked to the mall, and enjoyed the restaurants around the hotel. Finally on Friday at seven we drove to the embassy with Sophia and Carlos, I think at this point they were nervous to let me out alone. When we arrived there was the incredible long line again. As we entered the gate and approached security Juan held on to me tightly, he was seven. The guards and their guns scared him. Inside we waited in the big room again, I was interviewed again, paid my fee in American currency again. When they called my name and handed me the envelope that made you "officially" mine, I cried again. Christopher was coming home, with a smile and no idea of the battle that had been waged to get us to there.

After the hours at the embassy, Sophia and Carlos dropped us at the airport, we left for Miami at one. Once in Miami we passed through immigration and crashed at the hotel. Saturday morning at nine, we would put an end to this long road home. It had been just about 27 months since we had our driveway conversation about the possible. Now with one last flight and gathering of family at the airport, the possible would become life itself.

Many days I still don't know how much he understands of his own journey. For so long he was so conflicted about those left behind. We were too. We had no idea when this process started that he had two brothers and a sister in Guatemala. Same with Timothy, not until we returned home and read the reports in English did we know he had an older brother, about Christopher's age. Suddenly we understood why Timothy was so quickly and profoundly bonded to Christopher. He became the same brother he was taken from to go to foster care. We did not know.

I often wonder how it came to be that the women, who gave each of them birth, ever let them go. Grateful that I am she did, I don't know how she did. Kate and I have had many conversations about the kind of desperation each of them must have felt to let them go. Is there a greater love? Or is it pure and unadulterated selfishness on their part to let them go and not have to worry about how to feed or clothe them?

I want to believe it is the greater love, but I don't know. Most days I don't care. Really. I don't care to know how they miss them; don't care to think about how they might ache for sight of them. I am the selfish one that way. I am so grateful for their love and presence in my life. I am content to believe with every breathe I take that you were born for me, and that you are after all, exactly where you were meant to be at this moment.

The women who gave them birth were vessels to bring them into this world that God might answer my prayers. I am grateful to them and hope they understand too, you are where you were meant to be. Sadness is the feeling that creeps upon me when I think about and pray for them. Sadness for the pain they must feel in quiet moments if they let themselves remember you. It is my undying hope that in those moments the same God who brought you to me, soothes them and whispers into their hearts the truth of your being, and His plan. Comfort is my prayer for them.

Comfort was my prayer for Christopher as he fought his battles to be here with us emotionally. For the longest time he had one foot in each world. He so wanted to be here, so loved us, and was so tormented with the ghosts of memories still so alive in his young heart and soul.

One day after 18 months home he was riding in the back seat heading home from a birthday party. He asked about his mom in Guatemala. It was the first time he mentioned her, first time he mentioned them at all. All he said was: "I am never going to see my mom in Guatemala again am I?" Fighting tears the answers came from somewhere above, "Not for a long, long time honey." He cried and cried. Releasing the question and truths you could not hide any longer.

We knew the questions would come, knew the conflicts would be real, knew the walk would not be easy for him, or us. What did they tell him was happening? I suspect painfully little. He was five years old when he was placed in foster care. He had a life and history started there, and two years later he was here. Here in a place where nothing felt, or sounded or looked the same. Here where communication with us was a struggle, and life was full of plenty. Here where he could not be sure he would not be moved on again. He is just starting to fully understand adoption means we will love you forever; we will never let you go. You are home, we are your home.

Now on a different day, I listen again to you play in the yard, splash in the pool while you ride the rafts that are your cars and you shoot water pistols at imaginary bad guys. Over the five years you have all been home, we have logged miles of smiles and greater numbers of simple moments like this. Moments that are unspectacular in every way, except for the fact that they are ours. Ours together, ours forever. They do not realize yet what gems these moments that manage to stay in the storehouse of your heart are. These are the afternoons that build and bond the three of you to the two of us. They are the moments that create joy and sustain life. One of the things I hope I never take for granted, or lose is the way my eyes can fill with tears and throat choke with emotion at the simplest of times. Watching him score in a playoff soccer game where you are at your best. Sitting in the crowded audience of a fourth grade spring concert, you sing along to "What a Wonderful World" you look for me in the crowd and our eyes meet, you smile, I cry. Out of nowhere you tell me you are going to be the first astronaut to land on Saturn, sure baby, you can be anything you want to be. These moments bring me full circle in my thoughts and questions: I sometimes feel as though I am just an honored guest of their journey. That I somehow slipped, or took a wrong turn and landed on their path. Surely their souls sought me out, or drew me in to the journey, for in and of myself, I could not have earned it. Could I have?   Motherhood.

Chapter Two

Mom

It cannot be expressed and the words that try to convey fall incredibly short. Everyone who has known the loss knows and accepts the reality. Those who have not known the loss yet, accept too, yet for different reasons. One knows the pain, and knows there are no words; so silence suffices. The other lets the words suffice, knowing that asking for more definition can only increase the fear of things to come. Each is in anticipation of the soul wrenching pain of saying goodbye for the last time to their mother.

The highest call in my life has been the task of being part of her exit from this world.

With all the graciousness of the woman she was, so her leaving went. I intuitively knew when my brother called to say she was in the hospital with "probably pneumonia" it was not the case. I am both grateful and fearful at times for my intuition..

It started in October, it was over in July. The months in between were a single focused roller coaster ride. All of us wanted it to end in a different place. I knew it wouldn't.

From the first time I heard the word mesothelioma to the first Google search link I clicked; I knew it would not end with our desire. I was determined it would conclude in a miracle, I was just not sure how that miracle would manifest itself. Turns out the miracle would be broken up and scattered through the moments in between. There would be no celestial light, sky opening healing. As with most miracles and healings the food for the journey is buried in the routine. Throughout the grace of the journey the miracles were found in simple and profound moments of intense clarity and crippling pain.

Her and I talked about death. We talked about whether or not we really believed there was life on the other side. We decided there would be. We talked about what heaven would be; a garden for her, where she could have all her prior dogs, and no weeds. We talked about the lack of fear there. We talked about how she could let me know she had made it safely home. At least I know those plans worked out.

We all sat in the first row of chairs looking still in disbelief at her lying in a coffin; just one hour to go, the funeral, the burial, the end. The vase of roses that had stood guard at her feet was the focus of each of our attention, unbeknownst to the others. We each sat in our own stunned silence and watched and wondered if those roses were really moving or if grief and sleeplessness have taken its toll on our eyes. It took me only a few minutes to know it was just her letting us know. Why wouldn't she? She promised me she would. I asked and reminded her over and over again in our conversations to send me roses from heaven. She has, over and over again.

During the months of her leaving those conversations continued. She fought for some months, thought she might beat it yet, and then she knew too. She kept up a good fight for us. She wanted us to believe, she wanted to cushion our falls. She did an experimental trial in the late fall. She had surgery mid-winter, radiation in early spring, she was done in late May.

I remember the day I came in and sat on the chair facing her; she looked stronger than she had, I asked how she felt. She reported she was not as tired as days past with the radiation. Then she matter of factly said "I am going to stop the radiation. No more" it took a moment to sink in, and when it did it opened a floodgate in me that neither of us were prepared for. I broke to hear she was done with the fight. I could see and hear the pain in her voice as she said " Oh what have I done, I'm sorry" she was sorry.

Sorry that she no longer wanted to be poked and zapped; no longer wanted doctors to give her harsh realities or false hopes. She wanted to live out whatever time she had left, her way. She wanted to go to Wurtsboro one more time, wanted to tell stories and cherish hugs from her grandchildren. She wanted to build her spirit as her body deteriorated. She wanted to pack to go home. She was ready. She told me she kept thinking about leaving us, her home, her "stuff". "What am I going to do when Jesus comes for me?" she explained, "tell him I don't want to leave "my stuff"? We both laughed and debated the merits of eternal life versus "stuff."

Her sense of humor was only outsized by her concern for us. Over and over she told us that we would be ok. That she knew it would hurt but she did not want us to be sad. "Mom" I stopped her, "we are going to be sad, we are going to cry, it's gonna suck for a long, long time." Her eyes filled with tears. I went on, "How long did it hurt after Nana died?" "It still hurts she admitted, "After fourteen years I still miss her every day." "See I responded, what makes you think it will be easier for us?" "I know" she half pleaded, "you will feel like life will never be happy again, that you will always want to cry, but it will get better, it never goes away, but it does get better." I don't think I believed her. I wanted too, but I don't believe I did. As the years have rolled her words have proved true. It has gotten better, but it never goes away, "it" being the emptiness and longing, the sadness and the bitter sweet memories. There are so many bittersweet memories, of a lifetime, of those months, of her essence.

At one point in late May her doctor recommended she see a pain management specialist to help her cope with the increasing pressure in her chest. We all went; her, my aunt and me. None of us were particularly impressed with the man behind the desk who seemed to have a difficult time relating to people who were in good spirits.

As we sat opposite him he passed her a handful of prescriptions. She took them and flipped through; she looked at him and exclaimed, "This one is for Prozac! That's an anti-depressant!" A bit flustered the doctor began to explain that the gives it to all his patients in her "situation." Before he could finish the next line, she simply and emphatically informed him that "Just because I am dying, does not mean I am depressed!" With that, we all broke out laughing. The doctor was baffled as we stood and bid him goodbye.

We laughed all the way home. Imagine the nerve of him thinking she needed an anti-depressant! The memory of that slice of the journey makes me smile just because it is the very essence of her. Just because she was dying…

It did not mean she stopped being her, did not mean she had no hope for the future, hers and ours. She fervently believed hers would be lived in her heavenly garden. She so looked forward to seeing her mother and father again. "Whenever I start to think about leaving you guys" she told me, "I think about how good it will feel to here Nana's voice again. To hear her say 'Hi Nor" to know that I will never have this kind of pain again."

I think about those words now and each passing year I have a deeper understanding of them. In the months that followed their deaths we were cleaning out the house and we found an old cassette tape. One she had recorded twelve years earlier, before my brothers married, before grandchildren and the full move back to Brooklyn. On it she talks about how life is good, how we are all so good, how much she loves us. How she hoped that someday after she was gone we would find it, and have her voice saying our names, and how she loved us, as that was what she missed most from her own mother. I have the tape. I have only listened to it a couple of times in these years. Part of me can't bear it, Her voice makes the fact that she is gone all too real, some days the pain still takes my breath away.

I think about my sons, how she would love to hug them and make them laugh. She would sing silly songs to them, and tell them how handsome they are and how much she loves them. It saddens me that they never had those moments of her, only the photos and stories I tell them. It pains me to never have the joy of watching her love them.

One day they will be old enough to understand that the guardian angel that is Nana brought them to me through her departure from this earth. They will in their own hearts understand the silver thread that binds us together from the heavens to New Jersey to Guatemala and back. Somewhere along the way God and Nana wove a tapestry about us all and bundled us together for life.

If it is true that the love between parent and child best resemble the love of God for us, then what else would I believe about our story? How would I ever have the arrogance to believe that it was my doing that drew our lives to each other? The bonds are simply too strong and love too intense to be mere human made and grown. Out of the depths of my pain, came the joy of my sons. Her death and dying gave me a model of grace and another reason to believe.

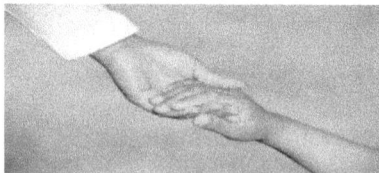

Chapter Three

Fifty & Me

There is an inconceivable date approaching.
November 10, 2009, my fiftieth birthday. Inconceivable.
How can anything so un-felt, be approaching so quickly?
I look at myself in the mirror sometimes and wonder if I
look fifty? I wonder what strangers see when they see
me. It seems like an odd thing to wonder, but my head is
full of odd wonderings. Odd wonderings and fond
memories are the stuff many of my moments inside my
head are filled with. Fifty? I remember my mother's
fiftieth birthday party, she had so much fun, laughing,
singing, dancing. She said she felt twenty nine; I feel the
same way most days.

When I let myself wander into fifty I have no sense of
dread or regret. I don't understand why some people fear
or disdain the passing of the time. I rather look forward
to the possibilities the years ahead hold for me.
Watching my sons grow into fine strong men. Seeing my
nieces and nephews reach the fullness of adulthood with
strong ties and joy filled memories.

I look forward to being one of those women who gives everything, but a shit about what people think of her. I look forward to the days when I can paint, write and create without thought to the clock. I leave the first fifty years behind with so few regrets, and face the next years with more blessings than I have likely earned. It probably sounds wacky already, but I treasure my gift of wisdom. It came to me thirty four years ago.

Each Friday afternoon a group of eight of us would gather in the small chapel on the sixth floor of Saint Joseph High School for the prayer group Ms. Rosin ran. I look back and realize fully I likely joined the group not as much for the spiritual exercise, but rather to spend more time with my best friend Bird, and Ms. Rosin. In clarity much later in life I realized I was likely in love with both of them. That aside, Ms. Rosin helped me tap into a deep, growing and abiding faith, both in God and less known to me, myself. We would fill that little chapel space with talk about life, about living and about how God might fit in. She challenged us beyond our adolescent arrogance and youth filled surety about how things were and came to be. One such meeting close to Pentecost we talked about the Holy Spirit. For all my years to that point in Catholic school, I don't think I ever heard anyone explain to me the place and depth of the Spirit. She explained the gifts of the spirit that they were just as alive and easily bestowed in 1976 as they were the same number of years earlier. She asked us to pray, and as we sat in meditative silence she ripped up a paper and on each little bit she wrote a separate gift of the

spirit…wisdom, courage, wonder and awe, prophecy….
Then she folded and tossed the papers into the center of the circle, asking each of us to silently request for God to infuse us with the one we randomly selected. I remember feeling that request. I remember unfolding the scrap of paper that held the word; wisdom. I remember being just a bit disappointed I had not pulled the courage scrap. I understood what courage was, I was about to embark on a life long journey to wrap my head, heart and soul around the gift of wisdom.

I carried that paper around in my wallet for years and years. I am sure I still have it somewhere. Regardless of the paper I have the ever present, ever evolving gift. It is there deep inside me as sure as each breath I take. It has served me so well, and been so true. It has been the conversation port with so many, so often.

One of the treasures my mother left us was a calendar/journal book of thoughts where on the page that held each of our birthdates she wrote us a note. Mine says:

"My Nor, you are the woman I would be. Your caring insight into all situations and seeing only the good- your easy solutions to problems have helped so many times"

I never recall telling her about the prayer group gift of the spirit. I am sure we never had conversations of my inward suspicions over the years that I was blessed with a gift. In moments of clarity or sparks of time, I felt the fullness of it rise up through my being and expressed in words. These words I type are the first of it I speak to anyone. There is no need to speak about it, it just is, and always has been. I am finally feeling unafraid to say I am blessed with a gift of the Holy Spirit that moves me.

I have a deep and solid faith in a God that loves me. I have never doubted the power of that love, nor the gift of that faith and wisdom. I guess sometimes I take it for granted. I wonder about people who lack it. Wonder how they manage to navigate the twists and turns of life without it. How does one manage to survive without a continual examination and connectedness to their souls? How can a life be claimed if lived without knowledge of self and creator? I don't get it. It is out of my scope. When I loosen my hold on the essence of who I am and who I constantly seek to become in spirit, I feel it. My days become clouded with lack. My eyes dim in negativity, and my heart ceases to seek gratitude instead of dread. I become a prisoner of my own being, rather than a participant in my own life. I have battles to fight within myself. Wars I have won fires I am still putting out. The gifts of faith, wisdom and love are my weapons.

I do not fear the approach of age. I fear that I will get to the end of my days and not be sure that I have done all I can do to use those gifts at every possible turn, in each conceivable situation to the best of my ability at that moment. It seems so simple to me that given the choice, one should always choose the kinder thing to do and to say. Simple is the concept that there is at any moment something of which to be grateful for; something that will move me beyond my limited sight of myself and situation.

One cold, icy and windy winter day I left my house for work and immediately dreaded the trek. I had to navigate myself across a city park covered with ice and exposed to the biting wind. With each slow step I took, I repeated a thought of complaint. Why didn't I have a car? Why did I have to work in the city? Why wasn't the path cleared? How I hated the subway wait and ride. How was I going to find the walk after I got off the train? In short, I had asked myself enough questions to be in a good state of self inflicted misery by the time I reached the subway platform.

Standing and staring off into the long stretch of dark tunnel I waited to see the first dot of approaching white light. I was still steaming with self pity when I was struck in the back of my leg. I spun to defend myself against whomever….. I was met with a gentle "I am so sorry." The woman who had spoken these sincere words continued on. She was swinging her white cane from side to side as she made her way down the platform. I was stunned; and filled with shame that eventually melted into enlightened gratitude. Who was I to pity my trek in the cold and ice when I could see my way cane free? In that moment I had something to be grateful for, something that would move me beyond my limited sight of myself that day, and many years forward.

Simple is the concept that there is at any moment something of which to be grateful for. I have had so many of those moments in the first fifty years of my life. I cannot begin to face the next years without the hope of more; more moments of gratitude, of wisdom and clarity, of laughing with abandon and knowledge of my God.

Chapter Four

Places

The same trees swing in the cool evening breeze. The same boulders guard the driveway; the same roads bring me to this place forty one years later. It is all the same, and it is all so different.

In the fall of 1965 my parents spent an outrageous amount of money, two thousand dollars, for a bungalow and the little plot of land it occupied on this mountain. It was white clapboard with navy blue trim. It measured sixteen by twenty four and in the wonder days of summer it was a castle.

Each year my parents loaded us in whatever vehicle my father had pasted together that year and we came here for summer. All week long it was my mother and the five of us in the bungalow. No phone, no shower, and a small television that brought us four stations when the weather was good.

When the weather was bad, the days were long and filled with books, coloring and otherwise; puzzles and often trips to Middletown where we could spend the day wandering the aisles of what can best be described as the grandfather of modern day Super Wal-Marts. Lloyds had everything from record departments to a bakery. It was our rainy day playground. Days were adventures and nights were sprinkled with shooting stars we could see from the porch.

These years later I watch my sons, nieces and nephews discovering the wealth of nature around them. They too, turn the woods into wild forests of the mystery and wonder that seems to only live in young minds. They collect bugs, toads and newts. They run from garter snakes, and swing from branches. They revel in the freedom of this place, never knowing the memories and grace that seeing them do so brings to my insides.

This place is in me. How do places become so much a part of peoples? What does it take, how does it happen that buildings, plots of land, landmarks become not only "over there", but critical to what is "in here" personal and indivisible. What separates one place from another? Memory. Moments. The continuity of time counted within the steadfastness of nature. The memories made in a place, move the heart; mine run far and deep.

In a reflection journal my mother answered the question: What is your favorite place in the world? Wurtsboro. I did not understand it then, I fully understand it now. The place was in her. The moments and memories she held were of those same summer days without the distraction of television, where she could see us run the woods, splash down in a pool, and discover more of who we were as "us" in the process. Her favorite place gave her the opportunity to do what she loved most, be with people.

The size of the bungalow never stopped her and my father from constantly inviting family and friends to join us for weekends or longer. The fact that there was no phone, no shower, no television, and no privacy was not a deterrent to the invite, or the acceptance of the invite. I remember one weekend we had 21 people in the house. Of those 21, the youngest was fourteen; we were a crowd of near or full adults, in a place that seemed to be made of elastic walls. The more people, laughter and love brought in, the larger it seemed to get. One summer my father decided the time had come to raise the roof, literally. He drew plans and recruited my uncle and two older brothers to create a second level on the little house. In the heat of two August days they ripped off the center section of the roof and began framing what would become four spaces. I hesitate to call them rooms. After the third day of work, it appeared a rain might fall. In the midst of rolling clouds and increasing winds my father and uncle threw huge blue tarps over the half finished roof, tied them down and hoped. It rained, and rained and rained for what was likely two, but seemed like forty days it rained.

During the afternoon of the second day the wind finally got the best of the tarp and the rain started to drip in from various locations above our heads. At a time when most wives living with a semi-opened roof, five kids of her own, a sister, brother in law and their three kids would pack it in and head out, my mother did not. Instead she handed out pots for us to see who could catch the most raindrops, telling my cousin she would probably win since she had the cupcake pan that could catch twelve drops at a time.

While my father and uncle refastened tarps, we caught raindrops and laughed, along with my mother in her now roofless and rain spattered favorite place. Eventually that project was finished and a ladder constructed that led through an opening in the floor above leading to the four spaces that housed more guests than I can remember to count over the years.

Much of the random visitor's time was spent baking and playing by the community pool during the day, and sitting on log chunks or the rocks that surrounded the fire pit by night. How many hours around the circle? In my mind's eye I can look across the smoke and flame in memory and see faces of friends, aunts, uncles cousins at various times. Smiling, laughing, telling stories, singing songs, spending time; and creating legacies around one crackling fire.

Everyone was welcome to her favorite place. There was always room for one more in her bungalow. It was easy and natural for her; she simply boiled another pound of spaghetti, grilled a few more burgers, stirred up another batch of potato salad. Everyone was welcome, so many came, and the collection of memories continued until they came full circle around in the times she wove through her life.

I visit that bungalow now; it has not been lived in for many years. It sits right next door, in the next lot over to the much bigger, much better, four season house they purchased many years later. Part of the roof is badly in need of repair, the floor slopes as the foundation shifts, the cobwebs and field mice live rent free alongside the energy and memory absorbed by the clapboard over the years.

It is all the same, and it is all so different.

Chapter Five

Am I Still Me?

I read this sentence buried in an article somewhere, and it produced one of those "Really?" minutes in my head. I could not decide if I agreed with Locke or not:"Philosopher John Locke, who said that a person recognizes himself as the same being throughout his life, in different times and place." Am I the same being I was 10, 20, 40, 50 years ago? On one hand I hope so. I believe we are born into this world with all the raw materials we need to become who our creator calls on us to be. What we make of those materials is really up to us, and how we blend our experiences, choices and those spiritual materials together; or not. I am the same being, as I have all that "stuff" given with the breath of life. It makes up the bedrock of me and I pray no force in or outside of me will erode it away. As far back as I can remember in my life I have always been in touch with the knowledge of a God that loves me; beyond what I learned in Catholic School. I have always been fascinated with the connections between people, how they ebb and flow and what a difference even a brief encounter can make in a life. I have always been creating something. Stories in my head, poems and paintings from my heart, there is a collection of "stuff by Nor" scattered throughout the places I have passed and people I have loved. From my earliest memories to today these are the things I recognize about my being.

Then on the flip side there are "those different times and places" and I would add people who undoubtedly have changed my life, and broadly, changed me. There are those people, times and things that have forced, coaxed, eased or danced me into re-shaping, re-thinking, and reviving who I thought I was before them. Does not just the act of waking and moving through a different day change a little bit of who I am? Does it not provide me thousands of little opportunities to express and improve that being defined as/in me? I think so. I think if I did not believe this, I would see no reason to hope for the good in tomorrow. Do I recognize myself as the same being as I was 10, 20 40 and 50 years ago? No Mr. Locke I do not. I am pretty sure I and all those who love me have helped me become a better "being." I don't think I am fully who God calls me to be yet, but I do know I may find some opportunities in this day to taking another step closer. I pray I see them.

Chapter Six

Where or How?

I sat there watching and as is often the case, my mind wandering into wondering: Where does the time go? And how does it pass so quickly? The passage of time literally makes me stop in my tracks. You're doing what? Your how old? When did you learn that? And where was I when you did? So many questions about the present becoming past, and moments of the past becoming a memory I did not even know I had until something or someone opens that door. Wandering into memories gives me perspective on today and beyond. It is the reminder that time quickly passes, that this day and moment will not come around again. I can be jolted into making the best of the moment I am in.

Yesterday in between soccer games, baseball competitions and school shows, I was sorting out winter clothing that would not fit anyone in this house again. Stuck way in the back of Michael's closet was a little tank top t-shirt with his favorite Cars character on the front. He laughed as he held it up and open, "This actually fit me?" It was no longer than the length now, of his shoulder to elbow. The moment and the question jolted me, yes that actually fit you once upon a time. Once upon a time you were small enough that I could lift you high in the air over my head and hear you laugh. Once upon a time you could not form those words to speak, but told me everything I needed to know with your deep eyes. Once upon a time just five years ago, that fit you. The exchanged reminded me that "once upon a time" is today, in all its ordinary-ness, today will soon pass in to the collection of days marked "then." What can I do to make it count for now? I took the little shirt from him, folded it, and put it in a drawer. Then I gave him a hug, cherishing the moment and feel of his little arms hugging me back.

Chapter Seven

Stupid Is...

I have to wonder about people who act stupidly. I know, I know, stupid is not a "nice" or "correct" word. I should not judge people, and honestly I try not too....but the reality is this: some people are stupid, senseless and foolish. Here is the dictionary definition of the word: stu•pid /'stup?d, 'styu-/ Show Spelled [stoo-pid, styoo-] Show IPA adjective,-er, -est, noun –adjective 1. lacking ordinary quickness and keenness of mind; dull. 2. characterized by or proceeding from mental dullness; foolish; senseless:

Can you honestly say you do not act in "senseless or foolish" ways once in a while? Sometimes I do. I admit it, sometimes I lack "keenness of mind." I am over tired, in a hurry, stressed, and my mind is not in the situation. I cannot decide which is more frustrating however, to come to the realization that I have acted stupidly, or to have to suffer through someone else's lapse into the state of "dullness."

For the sake of it I am going to go today with lapsing into my own stupidity. It means for me that I have done or said something that likely hurt someone else, even if only in the smallest of ways. That I have let circumstances or selfishness dull my mind and spirit to the point that my judgement and mindfullness of a person or situation has been clouded. I don't like this feeling. Really. I don't. I often go back and judge myself "stupid" and after I am finished chiding myself, I resolve to do better next time, forgive myself for being human and acting stupidly; and THAT is a really SMART thing to do!

Chapter Eight

Noise

My boys laugh and play with race cars and little Lego guys who run, shoot, and defend the universe. Lost in their own little world, they have no idea how much they make up mine.

Before they were here, in what I sometimes in my head call my quiet years, there were no racetracks to trip over, no bits of Lego pieces to step on barefoot and curse the creator of those sharp little edges. There in the quiet years there were no complaints of teasing or roaring laughter at goofy faces. There were no staring contests, no arguing over the details of games or life. In the depth of the quiet years there was no "Good night mommy, I love you too," or tales of being the first astronaut on Saturn. No games to cheer, no tears to dry, no homework to do.

It was peaceful, it was quiet, my time was my own for so many years. I prefer the noise of boys.

Chapter Nine

"Courage to change the things I can" that phrase from a little prayer has taken me through, and in many ways, transformed my life. It has been swirling around my head the past week or so. As I look to another time in my life that requires wisdom, courage and acceptance, I look for God to grant....

The dictionary defines courage as "the quality of mind or spirit that enables a person to face difficulty, danger, pain, etc., without fear; bravery."
The "without fear" part of that really kind of confuses me. Anything I can think of that I have faced in my life that was difficult, dangerous or wracked with pain....has also been with a tremendous amount of fear. Honestly, it was the fear that brought me to the point of willingness. I am quite sure that it is in fact fear that drives me to dig into the depths of my faith and call up all the courage I can.

Courage usually starts as a quiet, rolling moment of clarity of purpose. Then it dissipates into a shaky willingness to put one foot in front of the other, to take a small step, to make a small but meaningful change somewhere. Each time, each day, each moment that I am able to step through or over a piece of my fear, my faith and therefore my courage strengthens. Courage builds by action. It does not replace or dispel the fear, only quiets it until the moment my acceptance and faith are weakened once again by a look at the next moment, or task.

That becomes a dangerous moment. The very time I take my spiritual eyes off the right now and look ahead; is the same moment fear returns. Being able to live in a way that is courageous, is looking to me like the ability to live in the now. And that takes a great amount of serenity, acceptance, courage and wisdom....I know a little prayer for that!

Chapter Ten

Starting Anew

School is in today; and I guess that is a good thing. The start of a school year always signifies the beginning of something new, something not yet experienced. I so well remember the smell of those new black and white marble notebooks with the cover and pages so perfect and untouched. Carrying home a pile of books kept together with those silly rubber clip straps so my mother could cover them with cut up brown bags from Bohack or later, Pathmark. Everything was new again, the same place the same people. Yet, every year was a new teacher, a new chance to start over and make New Year's resolutions to get all A's or do all homework, or study more......just like the January ones, they were soon forgotten to the routine of the now comfortable.

The months would stretch ahead like an eternity to the next summer. In between was all the stuff of learning, of which I remember very little specifically. I remember the events of the years, first grade my baby brother was born, and I guess I learned to read. Second grade was First Communion and most of what I remember is the little faux fur jacket my mother made me to wear over my dress. I remember she wondered out loud who the hell decided to have First Communion in March this year? Third grade we rode a bus to another school while ours was rebuilt; and somewhere between the morning and afternoon ride I learned to multiply and divide.

Fourth grade I broke my foot, fifth grade the braces came off. In sixth grade I became friends with someone who is still in my life and heart today. There really can be something to that whole "BFF" thing. And so it rolled, each year something new, something doing, some learning that all started with the first day jitters, and the geeky love I had/have with new school supplies.

I can see, feel and hear the anticipation of the new year for my kids. They make me smile. They are so ready to start anew, and go back to the routine. They have all the pencils, notebooks, and markers. They have hand sanitizer and flash drives, locks for lockers and new lunch boxes. They are ready. I am not sure I am. I feel butterflies and a pull at my heart when I think about them entering that big building and having to navigate their way around, to figure it all out and make it work. Questions and fears run through my head and I try to remember: this is how it is supposed to be....as they grow I let go. I wonder what they will truly remember from this year. What days and moments and pieces of life will be implanted in their being and stay forever? I don't know, cannot even begin to imagine; for today just the chance to start anew in the frame of familiar seems enough. At the start of a school year or any another day forward we never really know which, if at all, of that particular day will last forever. This morning it is enough to know whether memorable or not; today is a gift, and in itself a new start.

Chapter Eleven

My Drive To Do

The time keeps ticking, the days keep slipping, and my list of things to do does not diminish. I know if I were feeling more spiritually fit this interference on life from my leg would be accepted as a good reason to slow, to rest, to pay attention. However I am not feeling the soul fitness- I am feeling the frustration of a child brat who cannot go out and play due to the fall of night. So I wait. Waiting for the sun to rise, waiting for the body to heal, and waiting for the next wave of clarity that all seems to take too long.

Impatience. If I had any smarts at all I would see this time as a grand opportunity to finally read through that pile of books, to work on my writing, to paint and dream. I wonder why I am so avoiding my own wisdom and voice. How is it that we come to a place in the day, world or life when we hush up the voice of our own wisdom and knowing? Responding to it as if it were a pesky child who wants our attention while driving....shhhh, quiet, later, wait a minute.....can't you see I am driving and need to focus? Oh, ok. But where are you going? And who will you be when you get there...I had best pull over now.

Chapter Twelve

I feel so uninspired. I keep wanting to blame the summer heat, the change of schedules, the crazy running and the drag of boredom. Yet somewhere inside I know it is none of the above, it is simply a quite normal and natural bout of "the blues." Or "situational depression" as it might be called in more psychobabble correct circles.

The end of June through the end of July is an awful time for me emotionally. It is full of anniversaries of pain and grief. Starting with June 28th when my father died, to July 8th, my Nana's birthday, July 19th, my Dad's birthday, to July 27th, the day my mom died. Each week of these five racks my heart with bittersweet memories of deep loves. I went and found the definition of where my heart has been the past weeks:

mel•an•chol•y   ˈmɛl ən̩ kɒl iShow Spelled [mel-uh n-kol-ee] Show IPA noun, plural -chol•ies,adjective –noun
1. a gloomy state of mind, esp. when habitual or prolonged; depression.   2.sober thoughtfulness; pensiveness. Gloomy state of mind, is not as fitting as the second entry of "thoughtfulness; pensiveness."   Pensive about the past, replaying both incredibly happy and devastatingly sad moments over and over. Looking for them to give me clues about the woman I see in the mirror, and sometimes stick my tongue out at. In my pensive, somewhat gloomy state I do find some strength among the clues. I find that as I play those moments, the good that is wrought out of pain comes clear. Funny how we usually only see that when we look back, and rarely while we are standing in the midst of it. I remember I am deeply grateful for the time I spent with my Dad before he died, particularly the last 5 minutes. In my memory I still see my laughing eyed Nana who was always an advocate and voice for me when I was too scared to be one for myself.

I delight in the memories of all those birthday parties with way too many people crammed onto the side screened porch singing happy birthday. My dad always seemed as embarrassed as he was thrilled to have that scene. The days and moments and months leading up to July 27th 2000, are too full of wonder and pain to even begin to describe here. It is simply one of three days in my life thus far that marked a clear before and after point. My world changed forever the day she died. I changed forever for the better for being there.

As much as I strive to live inspired days, I know the balance of them must come from the luxury that is indulgence in "a gloomy state of mind" and "sober thoughtfulness; pensiveness" Wandering into melancholy is not bad thing, living there however is crushing. As I allow myself to wander in, I must also know the way through and out. My exit ticket from the blues is gratitude for the moments, the lessons, the strength, and the love that all at once draws me in, and moves me out. Lack of inspiration is not lack of life; nor is it an excuse to pretend otherwise.

Chapter Thirteen

Teacher

Every year since I have been out of the classroom full time the end of June and the beginning of September catch me. I suppose I should not be, but I am surprised by it each and every time. I am caught at this time of year feeling like something is missing, more to the point that I am missing something; and I am. Being a teacher is the best job in the world. It is an awesome responsibility and overwhelming task. Teaching is joyful beyond description when done right, and devastating when attempted without success. I have been both of these teachers; sometimes in the same day.

Each year at this time I miss being in a classroom, miss the time and the packing, the fun and games, the sense of complete. Mostly I miss being able to look back over ten months and reflect. To think about how my students changed, learned and grew and how I changed, learned and grew with them. It was always with and for them. Always a dance and balancing act between the learning objective and the mind of a child. A constant stream of decisions to do or express the thing that would inspire and unlock, settle and motivate learning. Exhilarating. Exhausting. The list of things I miss about teaching children, and the list of what I don't miss are both long and varied. The single most important aspect lacking now is the relationship and connections with kids that touch your heart and soul for lifetimes. The wondering of "if;" if I made a difference, if I hurt some feelings, if I inspired, if I failed to see. If I taught well enough so that in each day each child knew I cared. Sometimes "if" is the biggest word in the world.

I will never know the full reach of any of those things, just one of the mysteries of a profession that is so complex, it defies reason. I will never know how my being teacher has landed on the hearts and souls of my students.

My students will never know how just being them has landed on my heart and soul. I don't think kids realize what an impact they have on teachers. How well we remember them, and how often we think of them. I guess what I miss in June is adding to the photo album of students in my hearts memory. Each June gives me a reason to step back and flip through those "pages" gives me another reason to be sure that of all the things I have been called in my life...teacher is one of the very best.

Chapter Fourteen

Five AM. I really like this time of the morning, particularly in spring and summer when the windows are open. Everything is so quiet; the world around me is caught between the dark of night and the light of dawn. My mind is caught between the dreams of night, and the anticipation of the day. In the in-between time lies stillness; and in this stillness often lies answers through thoughts and memories, random wishes and fleeting regrets. At this point of the day the regrets of yesterdays are fewest. I imagine that is because dawn brings such promise of hope, the regrets pale. Each of my days is a new foray into hope.

I hope I can do better today than yesterday, I hope this day sees me through to another. I hope....the five letters of the human spirit that make such grand and minor things possible through invention and change. The hard part of hope is putting the footings of action under it. Hope can move me, but it cannot stand alone. There is where so much of my hope for the days goes astray; in the actions that morph hope into change and change into strength. It is such a simple concept, a simple formula for most all of life: dream + hope+ action = strong living. Simple. Why then does it feel as though some days, some dreams, some hopes, are hopeless? Sometimes even with action, they fall flat and get thrown to the regret or forget pile in life. It is precisely the acceptance of this fact that gives me the new spark of hope to rise through this dawn and hope once again for better things in this day; as it is the only one I am promised...

Chapter Fifteen

In the summer of 1984 I had one of those moments in life that touch you so profoundly and deeply, you never forget them, and you never underestimate the power of a single moment in your life again. I am not talking about the moment you hear of a tragedy, or become one; nor am I referring to a life stage moment like engagement, graduation, wedding, etc... Important in their own way and place, yes, but not at the level of the awesome moment I am recalling.

We, my parents and one brother, took a road trip vacation to Bar Harbor, Maine. As was true on 99.9% of every other "vacation" with my father, we did not check into hotels, we set up tents. This trip was no different. We pulled into a campsite called "The Quarry" much after dark. We unpacked the car, sorted gear, and set up with a Coleman lantern barely poking a hole in the pitch utter darkness of Maine after sunset. We knew from the campsite map that we were on a spot that overlooked the quarry. We knew from the limited glow of the lantern, there was a fence and what was likely a drop off beyond it bordering the back edge of the campsite. After some discussion and snacks, we crawled into our tents and let the dark blanket our sleep.

I remember opening my eyes and the fact that I could see anything at all let me know it was at least dawn. I crawled out of the sleeping bag, and unzipped the "door" and there, there it was. Moving off my hands and knees and out of the tent, there was the moment.

There was the complete and consuming understanding of "Wonder and Awe." It was one of the few times in my life up to and since that moment, where what I saw took my breath away. The sun was just rising in the distance over grand and majestic mountains, and was throwing a glow over what seemed the entire Earth. For miles and miles and beyond eternity all I saw was rolling hills leading to incredible distant mountains all bathed in this light. Our campsite was at the top of a cliff where below exposed layers of pink and gray granite bounced the light back to the sun. Standing at the edge for hundreds of feet down, and miles forward, all the Earth was aglow with dawn, light, majesty and wonder. It seemed every thread of God's creation came together in this one place, and for me, in this one moment. I finally understood what was meant by the spiritual gift of "Wonder & Awe." In all my years of Catholic school no nun ever defined it sufficiently enough to name what I was seeing and feeling. Wonder and Awe, the gift of being fully aware and alive with the greatness of God around us.

That is my understanding of the gift. That is my moment of full knowing. I close my eyes I can still see that sunrise, I take a deep knowing breath, and I can still feel the power of nature and the love of God, all in a moment. And the fact that I can recall such an event and such knowledge at any time..... AWESOME.

Chapter Sixteen

Michael has a habit of beginning sentences with 'Mom, did you know that...." and he goes on from there. The topic of my oncoming enlightenment could be anything from the way to properly use the "squishy" part of your soccer shin guard to an interesting tidbit about the secret life he has away from me in second grade. Each statement is one of surety and confidence. "Mom, did you know that when Shane kicks the soccer ball at recess he makes it go curve by moving his foot like this..." "No honey I did not know that." "Mom did you know that the National Parks are all over and we can go to them?" "No honey I did not know that." "Mom, did you know that race car drivers wear special suits that make them not go on fire in their cars?" No honey I did not know that."

I often wonder what thought crosses his little mind when my lesson is done. Does he think what a fool of a mother he has for needing to be taught that? Does he think what a fine sharp mind he has? Or does he simply take joy and solace in the fact that he is caring and big hearted enough to share such useful information with me. I wonder if he feels sorry that I don't know these things? Regardless, I am waiting for the day when the follow-up to "Mom,, did you know that..." is not about soccer or monster trucks, or the antics of 8 yr old boys, but more like: "Mom, did you know that I am very close to finding the cure to _____ at work?" Mom, did you know that I still pray every day just because when I was little you told me it was a good idea to talk God each day even if you were not sure he was listening?" "Mom, did you know that I think being a dad is the best thing in the world?" "Mom, did you know you were right, my brothers are my best friends and always there for me just like my uncles were for you." These are the things I am looking forward to learning from my son, and the lessons of today just evidence to me that these are indeed coming.

I take such comfort in that thought, such joy in the
promise of tomorrows for my sons. Did you know that?

Chapter Seventeen

Waves

Each working day I exit Rte 78 and weave my way through the same neighborhood, making the same turns. It all becomes so routine. As I approach one corner, there is a routine that is not so mundane, not so taken for granted. There on the corner is the school crossing guard lady. Likely around 60, she is there watching over that corner and the children that grace it every day. Rain, snow, ice, heat, wind...she is always there. One day as I stopped at her command to let the kids pass, she waved me on and I waved back never giving it another thought, until the next day. As I passed by her station, I waved a hello. She waved back. We have been waving to each other every morning for the past three years.

She smiles, she gives me an enthusiastic arm flinging wave from her corner, and I do the same from the driver's seat. And I move on. Sometimes I think I should stop and actually introduce myself. Greet her with words instead of actions; let her know I look for her. Let her know that when she was not there for three days in a row this winter, I was a little concerned. I wonder if she wonders who I am or where I am going. I wonder if she gets concerned if she does not see me for a few days in a row. I wonder if she ever tires of standing on that corner. I guess I could stop and talk to her, ask my questions, and satisfy my wonderings. Nah. I don't think I will. I think I rather enjoy the idea of being just connected enough to this ever present stranger to wave. We participate in a mutual sharing of seeing each other; sometimes that is enough. Sometimes people just need to know someone sees them.

My final thoughts are only this: thank you. Thank you for sharing a part of my life journey with me. I thank you for reaching with me beyond and in to the everyday thoughts that keep my mind spinning, heart beating and soul thirsting. So many of the lessons we have to learn upon this earth are found in the simple joys and resounding hurts that we meet each day. There are two ways we can go with them, onward or downward. Attitude is the difference between the direction we take and gratitude is the fuel to keep us moving and learning on the journey. On my journey, I am still... not done yet.

###

About the Author

Noreen Gelling has been a writer, painter and teacher for as far back as she can remember. This book represents the first published work, with a second in process. In one form or another her time has been dedicated to created works of art and works in words. When not creating she is teaching. Her career spans twenty six years serving in a variety of capacities in urban education. She is a certified teacher and supervisor with an advanced degree from Fordham University and continued studies with University of Massachusetts and the University of Wisconsin. She resides in New Jersey with her three sons, and life partner.

Connect with me online:

nor@jukirocreative.com

www.JukiroCreative.com